COLLIN Y

CASTLES 1066-1500

David Linsell
Series editor: Christopher Culpin

CollinsEducational
An imprint of HarperCollins*Publishers*

Contents

attainment target 1

Questions aimed at this attainment target find out how much you know and understand about the past. Some questions are about how things were different in history: not only people's food, or clothes but their beliefs too. Others are about how things change through history, sometimes quickly, sometimes slowly, sometimes a little, sometimes a lot. Other questions ask you to explain why things were different in the past, and why changes took place.

attainment target 2

This attainment target is about understanding what people say about the past. Historians, as well as lots of other people, try to describe what the past was like. Sometimes they say different things. This attainment target is about understanding these differences and why they occur.

attainment target 3

This attainment target is about historical sources and how we use them to find out about the past. Some questions are about the historical evidence we can get from sources. Others ask you about how valuable this evidence might be.

Introduction

The picture below is an aerial view of Chepstow Castle in Gwent. It is just one of the many castles that were built in Britain during the Middle Ages. Before the Normans invaded England in 1066 there were very few castles. By 1200 there were hundreds of them.

Castles were sources of power for kings and barons. They represented the best in medieval engineering and they provide us with some of the most impressive remains from the Middle Ages.

As you work through this book you will find out why castles were built, and see how castle design changed. You will also learn something about the people who lived in castles and how the castles were built. Finally, this book examines why castles had declined in importance by 1500.

UNIT 1

Why were castles built?

AIMS

In this unit you will find out why William I and other Norman kings built so many castles and what these castles were like. You will look at several sources of evidence and learn why castles were such an important part of life in Britain throughout the MIDDLE AGES**. You will also find out how William gained control of the country by building castles.**

The Norman invasion and conquest

There were very few castles in Britain when William, duke of Normandy in France, invaded England. William landed at Pevensey in Sussex with a small army of 5,000 men. They were called NORMANS because they came from Normandy. William and his Norman followers defeated the opposing army – the ANGLO-SAXONS, who ruled England at the time and killed their king, Harold I, at the battle of Hastings in 1066. Although William had won the battle of Hastings and become King William I of England, he still had a lot of work to do before he could conquer the whole country.

As you can see from Source 1, William decided that the best way to gain control of the country was to build castles. Orderic Vitalis, a monk, wrote a history of the Normans. In Source 2 he describes how William and the Normans travelled all over the country, building castles. Some castle ruins from this period still remain today, like Clifford's Tower in Source 3. If you look at Source 4 you can see that future Norman kings also needed to build castles. They had built a large number of castles by 1200.

SOURCE 1
William I directs the building of a castle at Hastings in 1066. This source is taken from the Bayeux Tapestry.

'The king built a castle at Warwick. Next the king built Nottingham Castle. He fortified a castle in the city of York. When this was done the king travelled southwards, building castles at Lincoln, Huntingdon and Cambridge on his way and garrisoning them strongly.'

SOURCE 2
This source is from the *Ecclesiastical History*, written by Orderic Vitalis in the early 12th century.

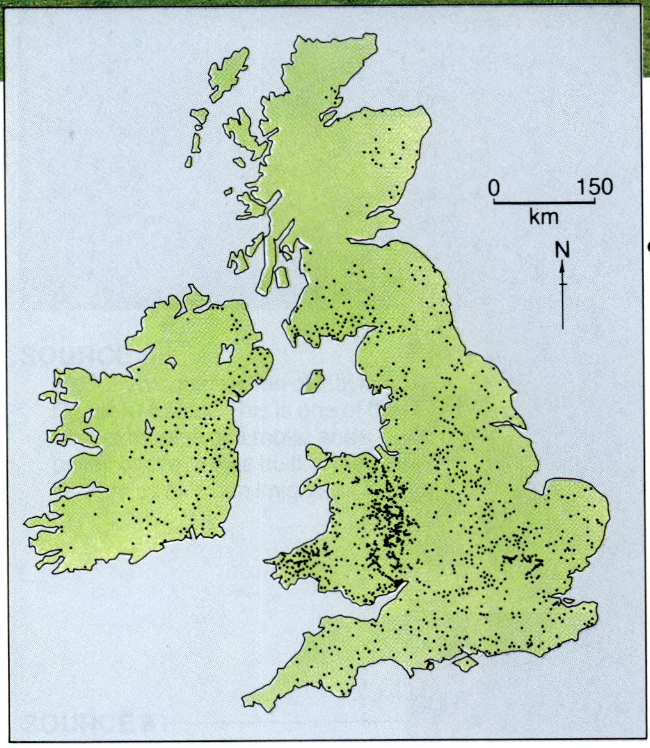

SOURCE 3
The remains of Clifford's Tower in York, built in the 13th century by Norman knights.

SOURCE 4
Castles built by Norman kings by 12th century.

1. How is the castle in Source 1 being built?
2. Are there any similarities between Source 1 and Source 3? Give reasons for your answer.
3. Use Source 2 to trace William's route across England onto a map of Britain.
4. What does Source 4 tell us about:
   - **a** relations between England and Wales?
   - **b** relations between England and Ireland?
   - **c** areas where the Normans did not go?

The impact of William's plans

If you look back to Source 4 you can see that the Normans built a large number of castles. Hardly anywhere in England was out of reach of a Norman castle. William built a large castle in London to control England's largest and most important town. As you can see in Source 10 this is built of stone. London required a much larger and stronger castle than a motte and bailey could provide.

The writers of the time disagree on whether William's plans were very effective. As you can see in Source 11, William of Jumièges believed that William I managed to gain control and rule peacefully. Other writers of the period felt that castles were less successful and the people very discontented (Source 12).

'The king carefully surveyed the lack of fortification of his kingdom and caused strong castles to be raised in suitable places, manned by a picked force of knights. At length the storms of wars and rebellions dying out, he now both mildly rules and even more prosperously and powerfully reigns.'

SOURCE 11
This source was written by William of Jumièges in 1072.

SOURCE 12
This source is from the *Anglo-Saxon Chronicle* of 1137.

'They sorely burden the unhappy people of the country with forced labour on the castles. And when the castles were made they filled them with devils and wicked men.'

SOURCE 10
The Tower of London. The White Tower, built by the Normans, is the central keep.

attainment target 1

1 Imagine you are the Norman knights who had Rayleigh Castle built (Source 7). Explain why you had it built and why it was built as a motte and bailey castle.

2 a Why did William build castles in the years after 1066?
  b Why were castles still important at the end of William's reign in 1087?

3 Read Source 11. What does it tell us about the short-term and long-term results of William's castle-building programme?

4 Does Source 11 or Source 12 give the most important results of William's castle-building programme?

How castles kept control

SOURCE 13

Chepstow Castle was built very soon after the Norman Conquest to control the mouth of the River Wye.

The Normans chose the sites for their castles very carefully. As you can see from Sources 3 and 10 they used castles as a way of controlling towns. The Normans also built castles to control important ports, rivers or roads.

Chepstow Castle, for example, in Source 13, was built to control the mouth of the River Wye in South Wales, while Mileham Castle was built to control the important road between the two towns of King's Lynn and Norwich.

ACTIVITY

Work in groups of four or five. You are a small group of Norman knights who have just come to this area. Source 14 shows five sites for a castle, labelled 1–5.

1 Give each site a score out of ten. Give reasons for your score.

2 Is there a better site not marked on the map?

3 Compare your results with other groups.

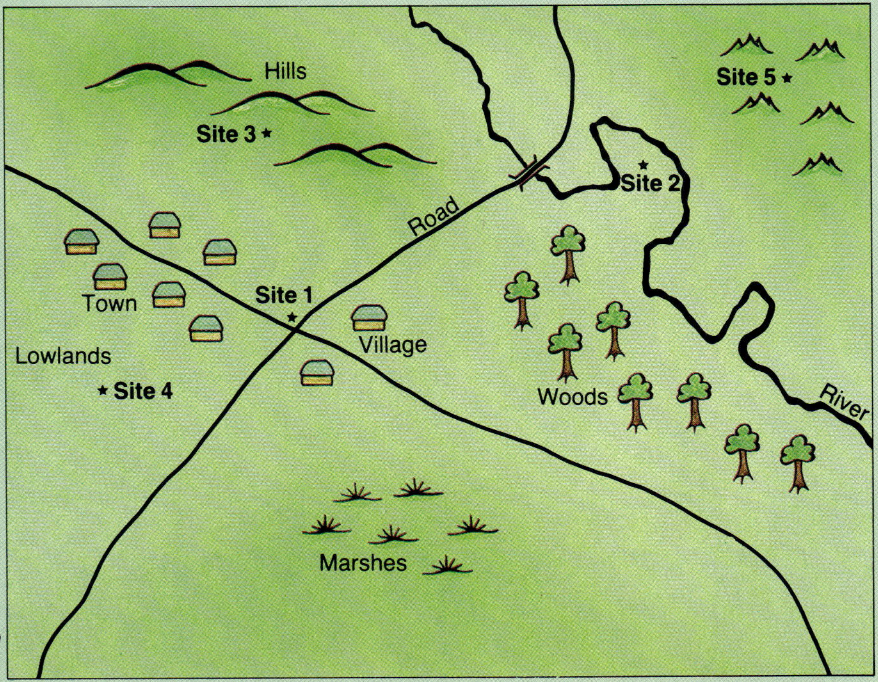

SOURCE 14

Five sites for a castle.

Castle design – an arms race

AIMS

In this unit you will find out how castles were attacked and how they were defended. You will see how changes in methods of attack and defence led to great changes in castle design during the Middle Ages. You will also find out how to recognise the period to which various castles belong. This should help you to identify any castle you visit and understand why it was designed in that way.

An ARMS RACE is where two sides compete with each other to produce the best weapons. Until recently the USA and the USSR were in an arms race. As soon as one side invented a new weapon, the other side would invent a new defence system to combat the particular weapon. Then the first side would try to improve on this. Therefore weapons and ways of destroying them became more and more complicated. You can see some of the weapons in this modern arms race in Sources 1 and 2.

In the Middle Ages there was a similar arms race over castle design. New ways to attack castles were always being invented. This led to changes in the way castles were built, so that the new methods of attack wouldn't work. The attackers therefore had to think of ways to defeat the new designs and so the race continued.

There were many different ways to attack a castle. In Source 3 you can see an attack on Baudas Castle in France. Source 4 shows the different methods of attack used by King Stephen I in 1136, when he tried to capture Exeter Castle.

SOURCES 1 and 2
Public displays of military strength in USSR and USA.

SOURCE 3

The storming of the city of Baudas in France, from a manuscript of 1400.

SOURCE 4

This source is taken from the *Deeds of Stephen*, written in 1150.

'Day and night, King Stephen vigorously and energetically pressed on with the siege of Exeter. Sometimes he joined battle with his men, by means of armed men crawling up the walls; sometimes by aid of countless catapults. At other times he summoned those who have skill in mining underground. He ordered them to dig deep into the earth with a view to demolishing the wall. Frequently too he made engines of different sorts, some rising high in the air to spy, others low on the ground to batter the wall.'

SOURCE 5

This source is taken from the book *History of King Philip* by William le Breton written in 1234.

'Weapons rained down on the knights like a hailstorm – stones, beams, jars of burning pitch and masses of iron. One soldier falls with gushing entrails, one with his throat cut. A thigh is shattered by a staff, and brains are scattered with a club.'

It can't have been very pleasant to have been inside a castle when it was attacked. On the other hand attacking a castle was also very dangerous. Historians from this period have left us many horrible accounts of what could happen to knights when they attacked a castle. In Source 5 William le Breton tells us about the massacre when Gaillard Castle in France was attacked. This was at the beginning of the 13th century.

1. How are the people in Source 3 attacking the castle?
2. In Source 4 what methods of attack did King Stephen I use to capture Exeter Castle in 1136?
3. In Source 4 how could the people inside Exeter Castle defend themselves against the methods of attack in Sources 3 and 5?

Wooden castles

In Unit 1 you saw how William I and his Norman followers had to build castles very quickly. Their motte and bailey castles were made of earth, with a wooden fence, or PALISADE. Obviously, these wooden castles could easily be destroyed by fire. As you can see in Source 6, soldiers who wanted to attack these castles soon found the best way was to try and burn them down.

'The main weapons used were the bow (probably with blazing arrows), sword and shield. Carts laden with dry wood smeared with fat were brought up to the doors. The attackers tried to set the wood on fire.'

SOURCE 6

This source written by Suger in 1130, describes Louis VI's attack on Le Puiset in 1111.

Stone castles

The obvious solution to this problem was to build stronger castles made out of stone, not wood. The Norman knights began to do this as soon as possible. They also built a much larger building, in stone, called the KEEP, to provide better living conditions for those who lived in the castle.

Source 7 shows the keep at Castle Rising in Norfolk. This is a very good example of a Norman square keep. It is large and looks very strong. The walls are thick and there were no doors on the ground floor originally.

1. In what ways would Castle Rising in Source 7 be easier to defend than a motte and bailey castle, such as Rayleigh Castle in Source 7, Unit 1?
2. Would it be more pleasant to live in a keep (Source 7) or on a motte (Source 7, Unit 1)? Give reasons for your answer.

SOURCE 7

The square keep of Castle Rising in Norfolk. The castle was built in 1140.

Attacking the walls

As you can see from Source 8 SIEGE TOWERS or SCALING LADDERS were often used to attack castles.

Scaling ladders had to be as high as the wall. They had hooks to grip onto the battlements. The idea was to climb the ladder before the enemy inside the castle could unhook it. If lots of people scaled the wall at the same time they stood a good chance of not being knocked back down again.

If you look at Source 9 you can read about some of the problems soldiers faced when scaling ladders were used as a method of attack. In 1346 during the siege of Caen, an English knight, called Sir Edmund Springhouse, slipped off a scaling ladder and fell into the ditch below. The French threw burning straw over him and roasted him alive.

SOURCE 8
One method of attack was to storm the castle using a scaling ladder.

SOURCE 9
An account of the Siege of Rouen in 1194, from the *History of King Louis* written in 1230.

'The besieging army were already prepared for battle. They raced forward from the camp and advanced against the city with scaling ladders. A most bitter hand to hand struggle took place on the wall. Weapons and bodies came into violent contact. Much blood was shed on either side. At length those who had proudly climbed the walls were thrust headlong down again.'

The siege tower

The siege tower was another slightly safer method of scaling walls. You can see a siege tower in action during the siege of Jerusalem in 1099 in Source 10.

Siege towers were always built near the castle wall. Any ditches would be filled in and the tower would have been dragged to the wall. However, this was not always as easy as it sounds. The tower sometimes became stuck in the swampy ground. Source 11 describes the sort of problems that occurred during the Siege of Carlisle in 1315.

SOURCE 10
A siege tower in action during the siege of Jerusalem in 1099.

SOURCE 11
The siege of Carlisle in 1315 from the *Chronicle of Lanercost* written at the time.

'Meanwhile, however, the Scots set up a certain great belfry like a kind of tower, which was considered higher than the walls. But neither that engine nor any other ever did reach the wall. When it was drawn on wheels over wet and swampy ground, having stuck there through its own weight, it could neither be taken any further nor do any harm.'

Battering rams

There were obviously problems when soldiers tried to attack a castle by simply climbing over the walls. Medieval soldiers, however, were full of ideas for other methods of attack. One of these ideas was the BATTERING RAM.

The battering ram or sow, as it was sometimes called, was usually a large tree trunk. It either had a flat head to knock holes or a pointed head to chip at the masonry. It was suspended and rocked on chains and was usually protected by a penthouse (shed) from the enemies' missiles. You can see a modern reconstruction of a battering ram in Source 12. The first written evidence of the battering ram in use in a siege is shown in Source 13.

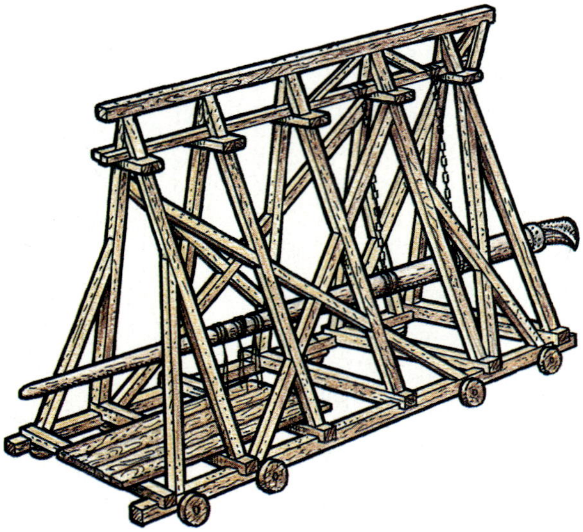

SOURCE 12
A modern reconstruction of a battering ram.

'Henry I arrived with a further reinforcement and applying the whole of his resources attempted to carry the town by various assaults with battering machines.'

SOURCE 13
This source is taken from Richard of Hexham's account written in 1138.

If you were a castle builder, how would you defend yourself against scaling ladders, siege towers and battering rams?

Siege mining

Another method of attack was known as siege mining. The soldiers would dig a tunnel until they reached the wall, usually at a corner. They would then dig a chamber and fill it with dry wood. When they set light to the wood the chamber would collapse and bring down the wall.

The only method of defence was to dig counter mines and fight underground. The sappers, as these siege miners were called, would find out where the mines were by watching the vibrations on pots of water placed on the ground.

Siege miners had considerable success. Gaillard Castle in France was thought to be the strongest castle in the world, yet most of it was captured by siege mining. You can see siege mining in Source 14.

If you were a castle builder, how would you defend yourself against siege mining?

SOURCE 14
Siege mine in action.

Changes in castle design

SOURCE 15
Bodiam Castle, built 1386 to 1388.

SOURCE 16
Skenfrith Castle in Gwent, built in early 13th century.

One of the problems with a square keep, such as Castle Rising in Source 7, was the corners. They could be easily knocked down, or mined. Also the defenders could not protect them very easily. One solution to this was to build round towers, such as Bodiam Castle in Source 15 or Skenfrith Castle in Source 16. The problem was that these round towers were simply not strong enough.

1 Which methods of attack could *not* be used against Source 15, Bodiam Castle?
2 What other differences are there between Source 7 and Source 15?

Castles without keeps

Some castles didn't have a keep. The palisade of the motte was replaced by a stone wall and the wooden hall built up against it. These were known as SHELL KEEPS. Source 17 shows the shell keep at Restormel Castle in Cornwall. In some castles the bailey palisade was replaced by a stone curtain wall. Towers were built along the wall to strengthen it. The first towers were square, but later they were either round or 'D' shaped. Source 18 shows the square towers in the walls of Framlingham Castle in Suffolk, a curtain-wall castle.

SOURCE 17
Restormel Castle in Cornwall, built in about 1100.

SOURCE 18
Framlingham Castle in Suffolk, built in about 1200.

Siege weapons

Attackers began to use weapons to fire missiles at a castle. They would try to break down the walls or even to kill the soldiers inside. One weapon was known as the MANGONEL. This acted like a gigantic catapult powered by twisted horsehair. You can see a modern reconstruction of a mangonel in Source 19. Another weapon was the TREBUCHET. This was an enormous sling operated by a falling weight. Source 20 shows a trebuchet in action during a battle. You can see drawings of trebuchets in Source 21.

SOURCE 19
A modern reconstruction of a mangonel.

SOURCE 20
A trebuchet in action.

Source 21a

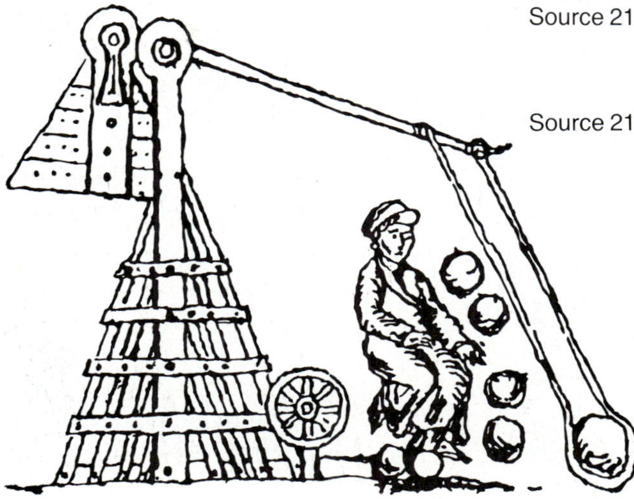

Source 21b

SOURCE 21
Source 21a is a modern reconstruction of a trebuchet.
Source 21b is an Arabic drawing of a trebuchet.

1. Compare the trebuchets in Sources 20 and 21. How do you know they are trebuchets?
2. Source 19 and most modern reconstructions of weapons are based on the drawings of a historian called Viollet-le-Duc (Source 21a). He produced his drawings towards the end of the 19th century. Do you think Viollet-le-Duc has provided us with accurate drawings of 14th century siege weapons? Explain your answer.
3. What are the advantages and disadvantages to historians of original sources (Source 20) and reconstructions (Source 21a)?

The concentric castle

Towards the end of the 12th century warfare in another part of the world began to affect castle design. The CRUSADERS brought back new ideas in castle building from their wars against the Muslims in Palestine. They made two important changes to castle design, to help defend a castle.

1 The crusaders did not build just one wall. They built a series of walls one inside the other. The inside walls were built higher than the outside walls. This meant defenders could fire their arrows over the heads of those on the outside. This gave twice the firepower. It was also twice as difficult to get into the castle.

2 The crusaders strengthened the castle gate by building massive towers either side of it. They sometimes built another gatehouse outside the castle, called the BARBICAN.

These ideas were used most successfully by Edward I, who built several concentric castles as part of his conquest of Wales. Harlech Castle, in Source 22, was begun by Edward I in 1283. Other concentric castles were built at Beaumaris and Conwy as bases for English soldiers to subdue North Wales.

SOURCE 22

Harlech Castle, begun in 1283.

Siege

If all other methods of attack failed the attackers would lay siege to a castle. This meant they would camp around the castle and stop any food from going in. In the end those in the castle would starve and be forced to surrender.

However, a siege took a long time. Most soldiers were only part-timers, who had to get back to their jobs on the land. The crops could not be left in the field to rot. As Source 23 shows, there was always the added danger that the friends of those inside the castle would come to their help. If a siege was successful the result could be terrible for those inside the castle. Source 24 describes how those in Rouen suffered enormously in the siege of 1418.

By the end of the Middle Ages castles could withstand sieges quite well. They were able to survive for over a year. The besieging army would have supply problems of their own by this time.

While the Earl of Mortaigne was besieging the castle of Lincoln, the castle of Nottingham and the castle of Tickhill were surrendered to Earl John who immediately sent word to Earl Mortaigne that, unless he quickly gave up the siege, he would visit him with a rod of iron.

SOURCE 23
This source is taken from Roger Howden's *Chronicle*, written in 1190 to 1192.

Meat and drink and other food
in the city began to fail . . .
The bread was nearly gone,
And flesh save horsemeat had they none.
They ate up dogs, they ate up cats.
They ate up mice, horses and rats . . .
Then to die they did begin
All that rich city within.
They died so fast on every day
That men could not all them in the earth lay.

SOURCE 24
This source is taken from John Page's account of the Siege of Rouen in 1418.

ACTIVITY

During the Middle Ages it was common for kings and barons to use manuals of war. They gave instructions on how to attack and how to defend a castle.

Work in groups of four or five. Each group should write instructions for one of the following manuals:

1 Defence 1090
2 Attack 1090
3 Defence 1300
4 Attack 1300

Remember the following important points:

a Your manual is for the Middle Ages. Do not include weapons from other periods.
b Wherever possible you should include evidence and examples. Do not forget to say where the evidence comes from.
c It may help you if you include diagrams and maps.

SOURCE 25
Carisbrooke Castle on Isle of Wight, built in 14th century.

SOURCE 26
Caerphilly Castle. The river was dammed to create a lake around the castle.

Castle defence

Source 25 is Carisbrooke Castle on the Isle of Wight. If you look at it carefully you should be able to see how well castles could protect themselves by the end of the 13th century. Look at:

1 The **CRENELATIONS** (along the top of the wall). These gave the defenders cover. Wooden shutters were often placed between them to give extra protection.

2 The **DROP HOLES** (the arches above the gate). At one time there would have been trap doors, which allowed the defenders to drop rocks or boiling oil onto the attackers.

3 The **ARROW SLITS** (in the tower). Notice the cross shape. This meant they could be used by both crossbows and longbows.

4 The bottom of the walls were sloped outwards. If you dropped a rock from above, it bounced out onto the enemy.

Which other sources in this unit have the same features as Source 25?

Source 26 is Caerphilly Castle. If you look carefully at it you will see that the castle has two entrances. The second entrance was often called the postern gate. This was designed as a way of escape. It also meant that attackers had to split their forces. Either gate could be used by defenders to launch a surprise raid on the attackers.

As you can see, by the beginning of the 14th century castle defence was very strong. Castles were still not impossible to attack, but it took too long or was too expensive. The balance of power seemed to lie with the defenders rather than the attackers. However, a new weapon, cannon, was to change all this.

attainment target 1

SOURCE 27

SOURCE 28

SOURCE 29

SOURCE 30

1 Look carefully at Sources 27 to 30. These sources are modern reconstructions of castles from different periods.

Match up the following captions to each of the sources.

a Rayleigh Castle. A motte and bailey built shortly after the Norman Conquest.

b The shell keep of Totnes Castle as it might have looked in the 14th century.

c The square keep of Rochester Castle built in 1127.

d The concentric castle of Harlech in about 1290.

2 Draw a timeline to illustrate how castle design changed using the text and sources in this unit.

3 Which of the following descriptions fits your timeline? Explain your choice.

a My timeline shows slow, steady change throughout the Middle Ages.

b My timeline shows some periods of rapid change and some periods of no change.

c My timeline shows that changes happened in different places at different times.

4 Look at Source 26. Explain the reasons for the design of Caerphilly Castle.

5 Which do you think was the most important feature of the defences of Caerphilly Castle?

Life inside a castle

AIMS

In this unit you will find out more about life inside castles and see that castles provided homes for a large number of people. You will learn that they were not just fortresses, but important communities. By looking at many different sources of evidence from the Middle Ages you will also find out how castles were centres for law and order and social life.

In the Middle Ages everyday life was centred around a castle. This did not just apply to barons and soldiers, but to other groups of people as well. You can see how important the castle was to everyday life if you look at Source 1. It shows a medieval landscape with a castle in the background. If you look carefully, you can see a little town clustered outside the gates of the castle. Many medieval landscapes would have included a castle.

It may surprise you to learn that women were expected to play an important part in the life of a castle. You can see this in Source 2. In the Middle Ages this would not have seemed particularly unusual. Married women were often expected to be involved in a battle to defend a castle, as Source 3 shows. The clergy also played an active part in castle life as you can see in Source 2.

SOURCE 1

A medieval landscape. This picture is taken from a picture calendar of 1400 and represents the month of April.

'The Bishop of Winchester . . . saw the walls and houses knocked down by the trebuchets. People begged him to take shelter because the mangonels and the trebuchets were destroying everything around. He then found the noble lady to whom the castle [of Lincoln] belonged and who was defending it as best she could.'

SOURCE 2

This source is taken from a history written by William Marshal between 1216 and 1219.

SOURCE 3
Women often had to defend castles against violent attack. This source shows women defending Acre Castle in 1286.

1 In Source 1, which seems to be more important: the castle or the town?

2 What do Sources 2 and 3 tell us about women in the Middle Ages?

3 Does Source 1 support or contradict this impression of the role of women?

4 In what ways might Sources 2 and 3 be surprising to people in the 20th century?

People in castles

Castles were very important places in the Middle Ages because they provided homes for the rich and powerful. The rich and powerful, however, needed people to run their homes and look after their lands especially when they were away from home. For this reason the castle became the home of a whole community who worked in the castle and on the land. If you had visited a castle in the late 13th century you would have found a family group, with their servants, rather like the gathering in Source 4.

The lord

William I and the other Norman kings knew that it could be dangerous to have all their powerful barons protected by mighty castles. The barons might have tried to become little kings in their own area, and even challenge the king himself. So when the king gave land to his barons, he made sure it was spread over a large area unless he was absolutely sure he could trust them. As a result, the barons spent most of their time travelling between their various castles with their servants. They had to make sure the castles were kept repaired and the soldiers trained and supplied.

The lady

The lady would often be left in charge of the family's most important castle. She would be expected to defend the castle in battle and run it as a home and household in times of peace. She had to keep a close account of the business of the castle. This was like running a small business. There were all the castle servants to supervise and all the farm work on the land attached to the castle. In Source 5 you can see adapted extracts from the accounts kept by Eleanor, Countess of Leicester.

The lord's children

It was usual for children to be sent away from home to be educated. They were often sent to live with another baron in his castle.

SOURCE 4
Dinner at the lord's table in a medieval castle.

'On Wednesday for the Countess and Sir Richard Chaplain of Kemsing: grain 50 kg; wine 60 litres; ale brewed; 420 kg of barley and 140 kg of oats.

Kitchen ½ ox from the castle stores. Fish 25p. For 700 eggs 11p

Stable Hay for 30 horses. Oats 140 kg from the constable's stores. Sent to the friars of Oxford 2½ kg wax

- Given to the barber of Reading for coming twice to Odiham castle, with one horse hired for his use, 13p
- For the expense of William the carter seeking one cask of wine at Staines, 5p
- For two pairs of shoes and one pair of stockings for the use of Robert de Valle, 7p
- For the dinners of the grooms and carters [while travelling], 2p
- For letters written by the countess carried to Kenilworth, 2p
- For baths at Odiham Castle, 1p
- For locks for the chest of the candle store, 1p'

SOURCE 5
This source is an adapted extract from the accounts of Eleanor, Countess of Leicester, for Eresby Castle in the mid 13th century.

1 In Source 4 find the lord, the lady and their servants. What are they eating and what are they using to eat with?

2 What does Source 5 tell us about the number of people in the castle?

3 Which servants are mentioned in Source 5?

4 What does Source 5 tell us about the journeys people took in the Middle Ages?

5 What does Source 5 tell us about Eleanor, Countess of Leicester?

The servants

The castle owner usually had a large number of servants to help run the household, when he was living in the castle, as you can see in Source 6. However, these servants followed the baron or lord as he journeyed from one castle to another. They did not live in the castle all the time. The most important servants were:

- **The steward:** a knight who was responsible for the day-to-day running of the castle.
- **The chamberlain:** a type of civil servant responsible for the paper work.
- **The chaplain:** he was also the castle accountant.
- **The chief butler:** responsible for the larder.
- **The marshal:** in charge of the stables.

There was also a number of other servants including: pantrymen, butlers, cooks, sauciers, poulters, ushers, chandlers, porters, bakers, brewers and farriers. Most of these had at least one boy or girl to assist them. Many castles at this time had a household of at least 150 people.

SOURCE 6

The lord had many servants to prepare and serve his meals.

Castles as homes

The living area of a castle had to accommodate a large number of people. How did all these people fit into a castle? How were the rooms arranged? Source 7 gives us an elaborate description of the living area of a French castle.

The life of the castle centred around the GREAT HALL. Some of these halls still exist today as you can see in Source 8. This was the most important room in the castle. Here most people who lived in the castle slept, ate and spent most of their time. The members of the lord's household were seen as part of a large family. Everybody ate in the great hall, seated at long tables. The lord's table was placed on a raised platform. The walls would either have been hung with tapestries or brightly painted. Tapestries added colour and kept out draughts. Green and gold were the most popular colours. The hall was sometimes the setting for great celebrations as Sources 9 and 10 show.

'The first storey was on the surface of the ground, where there were cellars and granaries, and great boxes, barrels, casks and other domestic utensils. In the storey above were the dwelling and common living rooms of the residents, in which were the larders, the rooms of the bakers and butlers and the great chamber in which the lord and lady slept. In the upper storey . . . the watchmen and the servants appointed to keep the house, took their sleep at some time or other. High up on the east side, in a convenient place was the chapel.'

SOURCE 7
This is Lambert D'Ardres' description of his castle – Ardres Castle – in France, built in 1117.

SOURCE 8
The great hall of Penshurst Place in Kent, built in about 1341.

SOURCE 9
This source describes a great celebration in 1388. It was written by an unknown writer and is found in *Froissart's Chronicle*.

'The queen kept to her chambers. She was no more seen that night. The other ladies and the king and the lords danced and revelled all that night till it was day and the morning. Then every person departed and went to their lodgings to sleep, for it was time.'

ACTIVITY

Use Source 7 to draw a side view of what Ardres Castle might have looked like.

As castle design became more complex the rooms also changed considerably. The food was originally cooked in the open, because of the danger of fire. With the introduction of stone castles separate kitchens were built. You can see how food was cooked in a medieval castle in Source 11.

For most people who lived in a castle there was no privacy. The only people to have their own private room or bedchamber were the lord's family. You saw this in Source 7. The lord's bedchamber might well contain the only bed in the castle. If you look at Source 12 you can see that the lord's bed often had curtains around it. This was to keep out draughts. Everybody else was expected to sleep on the floor and there were no carpets, just straw or rushes (see Source 13).

'During the Christmas festivities of 1246, Henry III's court ate, in addition to other supplies: 5,000 chickens; 1,100 partridges, hares and rabbits; 10,000 eels, 36 swans, 54 peacocks and 90 boars.'

SOURCE 10

The modern historian, J J Bagley, gives us an idea of the enormous preparation needed for a large feast, held in a medieval castle.

SOURCE 11

Cooking in a medieval castle.

SOURCE 12

The lord's bedchamber. Notice the curtains around the bed to keep the draughts out.

attainment target 3

1 Compare Source 8 with Sources 9, 10, 11 and 12. Which is the most useful source if you want to find out about the inside of a medieval castle?

2 What are the advantages and disadvantages of Sources 8, 9, 10 and 11 if you want to find out about medieval castles?

3 Source 10 is taken from a book written by a modern historian. What would you want to know about Source 10 in order to judge its reliability?

attainment target 1

4 In what ways was living in a castle at the end of the Middle Ages different from living in a motte and bailey castle?

5 Select four sources from Units 1 to 3 to illustrate the following topics: castles in war; castles at peace; castles for the rich and castles for the poor. Add two sentences of your own to explain your choice.

SOURCE 13
Most members of the household slept on the floor of the great hall.

By the later Middle Ages there were more private rooms in castles and more comfort. The lord's family rarely ate in the hall, except on special occasions. They had their own, cosier, lighter rooms. More rooms were gradually added over the years, including guest rooms. These might have included:

- **A chapel** where the lord and lady would be expected to pray at least once a day.
- **A cellar**
- **A wardrobe or large cupboard** where valuable items such as spices, cloth and silver plate were locked away. One of the most prized spices was saffron. It took 150,000 crocuses to make 1 kg of saffron. In the 13th century it cost over £1.00 for 1 kg at a time, when a servant could expect to earn 50p a year.
- **The privy or** GARDEROBE (this was usually over a hole in the wall), which usually emptied directly into the moat.

The importance of castles

The king gave his barons many social and legal responsibilities for their own particular area of the country.

Law and order

A baron was usually made responsible for keeping law and order in his county or area, as Source 14 shows. He would hold a law court in his castle. It was common for any punishments to be carried out at the castle as you can see in Source 15. Often the local prison would be in the dungeon of a castle.

> 'I grant to my barons of Hastings their honours in my court, and their freedoms. I order that they shall take care of my peace and justice. In return for their freedoms they shall provide me each year with 20 ships for 15 days at their own cost.'

SOURCE 14
This source is taken from the *Charter of Henry II*, 1154 to 1158.

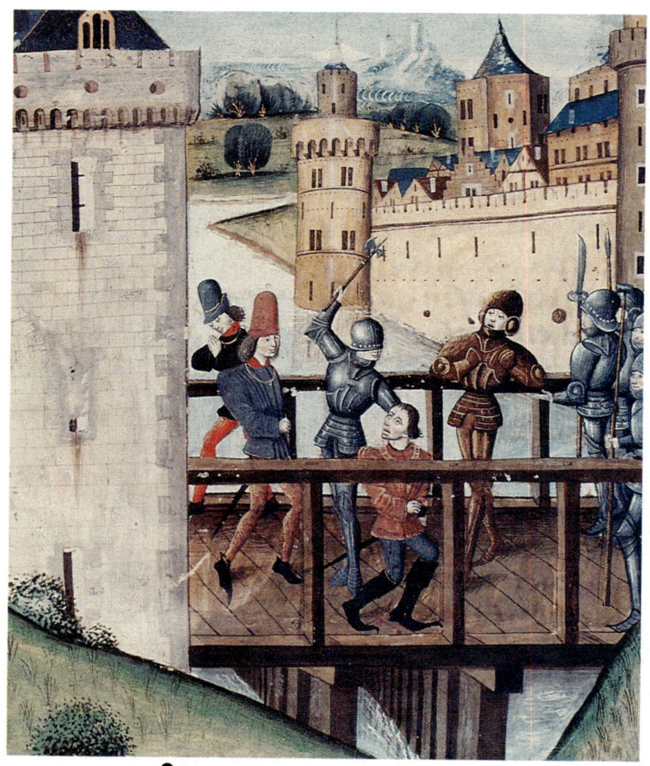

SOURCE 15
Execution of John the Fearless at Montereau Castle in 1419.

Tournaments

As you saw in Source 9, large social gatherings took place in castles. One of the most popular ways to bring lords, barons and their families together was at a tournament. Men were trained to fight and a tournament was a type of mock battle. It kept knights in training when there wasn't a war going on and it stopped them from making trouble.

In the early Middle Ages the tournament usually consisted of a melée as you can see in Source 16. In a melée a large group of knights fought each other. The problem with a melée was that knights were often hurt and real battles would break out. By the later Middle Ages the joust was more common. Here individual pairs of knights fought each other. You can see a joust in Source 17. War, battles and fighting were important activities for young knights. Tournaments like these allowed them to show off their skill.

SOURCE 17

A joust in the later Middle Ages. Banquets and many other forms of entertainment would also take place at a tournament.

SOURCE 16

A melée at a tournament in the early Middle Ages.

UNIT 4

How were castles built?

AIMS

In this unit you will find out how castles were built and who built them. It explains some of the similarities and differences between building today and building in the Middle Ages. A variety of sources will help you understand the huge scale on which castles were built during the Middle Ages.

Building sites

In 1179 William of Sens, a famous French architect, was in charge of rebuilding Canterbury Cathedral. William was getting ready to build the VAULT, and was standing on wooden scaffolding, high above the ground, when he had a serious accident. Gervais, a monk who lived in Canterbury at the time, witnessed the accident and describes what happened in Source 1. William fell from his scaffolding when the beams broke under his feet. He was not killed but was very badly injured and returned to France. Accidents were commonplace on medieval building sites as you can see from Sources 2 and 3. Building sites were dangerous and noisy places with hundreds or even thousands of workmen.

SOURCE 1
This source is taken from the *Anglo-Saxon Chronicle*.

'William was, at the beginning of 1179, in the act of preparing with machines for the raising of the great vault when suddenly, the beams broke under his feet and he fell to the ground, stones and timbers accompanying his fall, from the height of . . . 50 feet.'

SOURCE 2
Accident on a medieval building site. This is taken from an Austrian bible from about 1250.

SOURCE 3

Accident on a medieval building site. This is also taken from an Austrian bible from about 1250.

1. What can we learn from Sources 1 to 3 about how medieval builders worked?
2. Why do you think there were so many accidents on medieval building sites?

Building techniques

Castle builders were very skilled. Their castles had to be strongly built in order to stand up to the battering they might receive in an attack. This is why so many castles from this period are still standing today even if they are in ruins.

However, building technology had not changed since Roman times. The builders didn't have any modern machines like cement mixers, electric stone cutters, pneumatic drills, powered cranes or earth diggers. Therefore most stone castles took at least seven years to build. There were a few exceptions: Richard the Lion Heart, for example, built Gaillard Castle in France in less than three years, but it took Edward I over 25 years to build Caernarvon Castle.

ACTIVITY

Work in pairs. Here are some descriptions of the various jobs involved in building a stone castle. However, the order in which they had to be done has been jumbled up. Sort out the descriptions into the correct order. You can see most of these jobs in Sources 4 and 5.

SOURCE 4

Stone cutters at work.

1 The site was cleared. Sometimes masons had to chisel away at solid rock. If the castle was to be built in a town it might have been necessary to knock down houses.

2 The foundations were dug, preferably into rock. Otherwise rubble and mortar (cement) would be laid, often to a considerable depth.

3 The timber was cut (it was used for beams, scaffolding, workshops and machines).

4 The stone was quarried. It was usually cut roughly to shape at a quarry near the castle, because it was very expensive to move stone over a long distance. It was then carved on site (see Sources 4 and 5).

5 Workshops were built.

6 The walls and towers would be built. Stones were raised from the ground using a crane (Source 4) or a WINDLASS, a large wooden wheel inside which men walked (like a hamster's wheel). An inner and outer wall would be made from carefully cut stone called ashlar. The area in between the walls would be filled with rubble and cement (see Sources 4 and 5). A maximum of only three metres could be built in a year to allow the mortar to dry. The top was covered with straw to keep the frost out and left over the winter.

7 Wooden scaffolding was used. As the building rose so did the scaffolding. It was either placed in a spiral around the towers or as shelves connected to the wall, but not the ground (see Source 5).

8 The outside walls would be white washed.

9 The hall, kitchen, chapel and other domestic rooms would be added. These might be inside the towers or against the walls.

The castle builders

Castle builders consisted of two groups.

1 **Skilled workers**, who were masons and carpenters.

2 **Unskilled labourers** who were mainly diggers.

SOURCE 5
Masons, diggers and stone cutters at work.

10 The drawbridge, portcullis and wooden walkways would be added.

11 Wooden roofs would be added to the towers, which were often covered in lead (see Source 5).

12 A temporary wooden hall would be built to house the lord, his family and the castle builders.

13 The ditches and moats were dug. They were v-shaped and covered in clay to stop them from collapsing. The soil would be used to build the mound and ramparts. The mound was often reinforced with layers of rock and clay.

14 The plans were drawn up. The king's permission was usually needed.

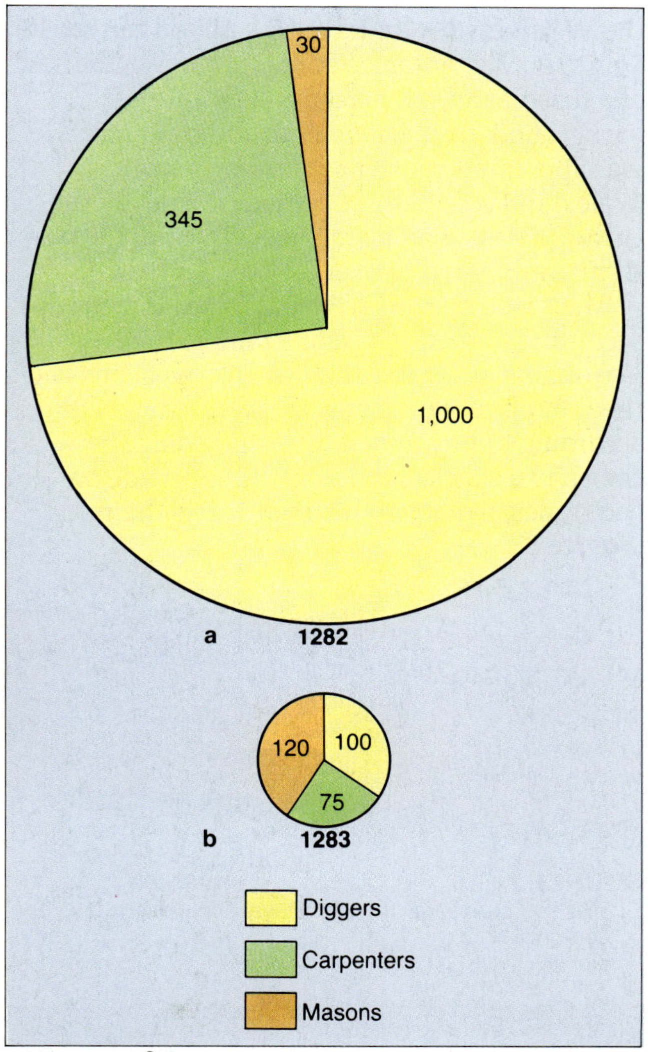

SOURCE 6
a Masons, carpenters and diggers who worked on Edward I's Welsh castles in 1282.
b Masons, carpenters and diggers who worked on Edward I's castles in 1283.

1 Look at Source 6. How many masons, carpenters and diggers were there by 1283?

2 In Source 6 how many workers were needed altogether?

3 In Source 6 why were there more diggers and carpenters needed at the beginning than masons?

Masons

All the workers had to be organised. They had to be hired, paid and kept supplied with materials. This was the job of the MASTER MASON. The master mason was a mason who worked in stone, who was also the architect. The most famous master mason was Master James of St George. He was responsible for building many of the Welsh castles for Edward I, as you can see in Source 7. Master James of St George was the son of a mason and came from a fairly humble background, from Savoy in southern France. He was appointed 'master of the king's works in Wales' and constable of Harlech Castle. By the early 1300s he had an income, which in today's terms, amounted to over £250,000 a year.

The stone masons were organised into groups according to their jobs. For example the BANKER masons cut the stones and the FIXER masons laid them in place. These masons were often paid according to how much work they did. They each had a special mark which they made on the stones, to show which work was theirs (Source 8).

'8 April. To Master James in payment of his wages for 17 days . . . 17s. To the same James going into Wales to oversee the works of the castles there, for his wages and expenses for 29 days . . . 58s.'

SOURCE 7
This source is taken from the Royal Accounts, late 13th century.

SOURCE 8
Each mason made a mark on his stones.

If you look at Sources 9, 10 and 11 you can see the way the masons did their jobs. The banker masons worked in a shed, protected from the weather. When the walls were low, carved stone was carried, or taken in a wheel barrow to the place where it was needed. As the walls grew higher, various lifting devices were used to raise the stone, or the mortar. Great care had to be taken to see that the walls were exactly vertical, and rows of stone exactly level.

SOURCE 9
A rich patron is shown over a building site by a master mason.

SOURCE 10
Medieval builders at work. Note the plumb-level, hoist and axes used by mason and carpenter.

attainment target 3

1. Imagine you are the rich patroness in Source 11 or the patron in Source 9, who is paying a visit to the site. When you get home you have to describe what you saw to the rest of your family. What do you say?
2. Use the sources in this unit to describe the skills that masons had to have.
3. Use the sources in this unit to explain why masons were paid so much more than labourers.
4. Which is the most useful source in this unit to describe the job of the medieval mason?
5. Use this unit and unit 3 to describe four jobs of working people in castles.

Labourers

If you look back to Source 6 you can see that a large number of diggers were needed. Their work must have been backbreaking. They had very few tools, mostly spades, axes, buckets and wheel barrows. At the time of the Norman Conquest William I forced men to work unpaid on castle building. By the time of Edward I's Welsh campaign in 1282 they were paid, but could still be forced to work anywhere in the country. This is called CONSCRIPTION. Diggers also had a reputation for bad behaviour. As you can see in Source 12, it was often difficult to keep them under control.

SOURCE 12

This source is taken from the minutes of a meeting of royal officials in 1289.

'Control of the diggers is to be left up to you, provided that whoever is sent to seek them is their chief leader and other constables are appointed under him.'

SOURCE 11

A rich patroness looks over a site, where a cathedral is to be built.

Carpenters

When you looked at Source 6 you might have been surprised that so many carpenters were needed. If you look at castle ruins today you can see what the diggers and masons did, but it is more difficult to see the work done by the carpenters. Most of the wood has either rotted away or been removed. This often included buildings such as the hall and stables, and many of the walkways, floors and roofs.

If you look at Source 13, you can see what a large wooden building in a medieval castle might have looked like.

SOURCE 14
Carpenters and their tools.

SOURCE 13
Westminster Hall.

1. Look carefully at Source 14. Write down as many different uses of wood as you can find.
2. Describe the tools the carpenters used in Source 14. In what ways are the tools different from those used by modern carpenters?
3. Make a list of the different types of workers you would find on a medieval building site. Which of these jobs would you most like to have done? Why?

Smiths

Every castle building site also had a number of smiths. Not much metal was used in the castle itself, but the smiths were essential to look after the tools of the diggers, masons and carpenters. Most of the tools were made of wood, but the edges of spades, saws and chisels were made of metal. Smiths not only made the tools, but also kept them regularly sharpened. All the workers therefore depended on the skill of the smiths.

Castle building on a vast scale

Source 6 shows that Edward I brought large numbers of workers to Wales to build his new castles. He needed to build several castles very quickly in order to control the Welsh. This was a huge operation as you can see from Source 15. Edward I built Caernarvon Castle in the late 13th century (see Source 16).

SOURCE 15

This source shows the important dates in the building of Caernarvon Castle.

JUNE 1283	Timber palisade transferred from Rhuddlan Castle. New moat dug (north side) costing 50p. Twenty ship-loads of timber arrived.
JULY 1283	Houses demolished to clear site. Forty two carpenters built eight-room hall for visit of Edward I and his court. Lawn laid for queen.
AUGUST 1283	Sheriffs of Shropshire and Staffordshire ordered to send 300 good masons.
1284	Rock on site levelled and foundations laid.
1285	Lead sent from Bristol for roofs.
1292	Castle wall completed to a height of about 10 metres. Eagle Tower first lived in. Towers and walls on northern side started.
1294	The Welsh rose in revolt and sacked the castle.
1295	Building resumed under the control of Master Walter of Hereford.
JUNE 1295	Seventy masons, 18 quarriers, eight carpenters, eight smiths, 175 labourers and nine clerks working on the castle.
1305	Philip the carpenter was paid £22 to joist a three storey tower. £8 was paid for two drawbridges.
1312	Wall walks, stables, bakery and brewhouse were finished.
1317	Turrets completed on Eagle Tower.
1320	Smiths forged hooks, bars and staples for large windows.
1330	Work finally halted with gates and towers unfinished.

SOURCE 16
Caernarvon Castle.

Between 1277 and 1304 Edward I spent over £12,000 on Caernarvon Castle. In the same period he spent over £78,000 building all his other Welsh castles. This was an enormous amount of money. It is very difficult to translate this enormous sum to modern values. It amounted to more than Edward's entire tax revenue for a year. Today that is over £200 million. Caernarvon Castle cost Edward I so much money that he could not afford to fight the Scots. Nevertheless, he regarded it as good value because it cost him nearly twice as much to send out an army to try and conquer Wales.

1 Compare Source 15 with the descriptions on pages 34 and 35. How far does Source 15 match up with the jobs in the activity and the order in which you placed them?

2 What aspects of castle building are missing from Source 15?

3 What extra information about castle building does Source 15 give you?

4 Describe what you might have seen at Caernarvon Castle (Source 16) in the following years: 1284, 1293 and 1330.

The decline of castles

AIMS

In this unit you will find out more about when castles declined and why they declined. Modern historians have different ideas about why castles declined. You will look at some of their ideas, and then see how far the evidence supports them.

What are castles like today? Some of the earliest motte and bailey castles have almost completely disappeared. Only a small mound in a field shows the remains of a motte. Some castles are in ruins, like Ludlow Castle in Source 1. Many of these ruined castles are open to the public. They have carefully-mown grass and labels to show each part of the ruin. Some castles no longer look like castles, but have been turned into large houses, or even palaces, like Windsor Castle in Source 2. In all these cases it is hard to imagine what the original castle looked like. Obviously a great change happened to all these castles at some time in their history. When did this happen and why?

Until the 14th century castles were like small villages. If you look at Source 3, however, you can see that some aspects of castle life had already begun to change. The great hall had declined in importance and was no longer the centre for everyday events or large social gatherings.

As we have already seen many different types of castles were built. Each castle had a different fate. Some castles were knocked down, some fell into ruins, some were restored. All were totally changed.

SOURCE 1
Ludlow Castle.

SOURCE 2
Windsor Castle, which has been turned into a large house.

'Wretched is the hall each day in the week. There the lord and lady liketh not to sit. Now has she such a rule to eat by themselves in a privy parlour for poor men's sakes, or in a chamber with a chimney, and leave the chief hall, what was made for meals, for men to eat in.'

SOURCE 3
This source is from *The Vision of Piers Plowman* by William Langland, written in about 1362.

1. What has happened to the original castles in Sources 1 and 2?
2. What is Langland complaining about in Source 3?
3. In Source 3, why did the lord and lady prefer 'a chamber with a chimney' to the hall?
4. Source 3 suggests one reason why the old way of life in castles was changing. Do you think this is the main reason for the decline in castles?

Why castles declined

In this book you have looked at a variety of different types of castle. There were, of course, hundreds more castles in Britain in the Middle Ages. Each castle had its own story and its own reasons for decline, but hundreds of stories are not much use to us when we try to find a pattern in the past. Historians try to explain this pattern to us. They examine lots of different examples and look for what they have in common.

Modern historians have many ideas which might explain the decline of castles. One theory is that all the ruined castles were destroyed in wars or sieges. However, if you look at Source 5 you can see that this is not a popular idea. Another idea is that the nature of war itself changed with the use of cannon and gunpowder in the 11th century. By the end of the Middle Ages life had become more peaceful. Source 4 shows King Henry IV (1399 to 1413) with his followers, not in armour, but in fashionable clothing. It was also very expensive to rebuild or restructure a castle so that it could stand up to cannon fire. Source 6 focuses on these factors.

If you look back to Source 3, it suggests another reason for the decline of the castle: a desire for comfort. Most historians feel that all these factors contributed to the decline of castles (Source 7).

'Sieges did not produce the ruins we see today. They were caused by the determination of the king to raze (destroy) a castle, which might disturb the peace of the realm.'

SOURCE 5
An extract from *A Baronial Household of the 13th century*, written by the modern historian M Wade Labarge.

Castle building, maintenance and repair were expensive, and many castles went out of use for financial reasons.

SOURCE 6
An extract from *Norman Castles in Britain* written by the modern historian D Renn.

'The demand for more space and greater comfort becomes increasingly important in the plan of new castles . . . internally they were houses. Their military value had declined largely because of changes in warfare, which was being waged by larger, more professional armies who conducted their battles in the field. The king settled down in and around London. There was a corresponding lessening in the need for royal castles.'

SOURCE 7
An extract from *The High Middle Ages*, written by the modern historian T Rowley.

SOURCE 4
Henry IV and his followers.

1 Look at Sources 4 to 7 and draw up a list of the reasons why castles declined.

2 Different historians give different reasons for the decline of castles. Does this mean that only one of the historians is right?

Evidence for the decline of castles

Historians have based their ideas in Sources 4 to 7 on their study of the evidence available. Tattershall Castle in Lincolnshire was partly rebuilt between 1434 and 1435. Source 8 is an extract from the building accounts. You can see that to alter or rebuild a castle was very expensive and involved a lot of work.

The use of cannon spelt the end for castles. Although early cannon could only fire a stone cannonball a short distance (about 300 metres), they were still very destructive.

There were no castles built up to this time that were able to withstand cannon fire. New styles of forts were built to stand up to gun fire, but these were very expensive (see Source 10).

Sources 9 and 10 show two castles built at the end of the Middle Ages. One castle was built for comfort and one was built to withstand cannon fire. Is it easy to tell which is which? It was not always possible to combine both these requirements at this time.

SOURCE 8

Building expenses at Tattershall Castle, 1434 to 1435.

'Renewing of chimney made this year £5.06
Various carpenters engaged on carpentry during the time £14.92
Robert Kerver and his mate working on the ceilings of the parlour £2.72
John Plommer and his servant, for various plumbing jobs £1.33
Wages of various carters with their carts carrying stone, brick, sand and such like .... £10.35'

SOURCE 9

Castle Craigievar in Grampian, completed in 1626.

SOURCE 10

A view of Deal Castle, built in 1539. The castle was built to withstand cannon fire.

The stories of two castles

So far we have looked at evidence from lots of different castles to see how and why castles declined. In Sources 11 and 12 we will look at the brief history of two particular castles, Windsor Castle and Tantallon Castle, to see what happened to them.

1067 Motte and bailey castle built
1175 Round tower built
1236 Became the king's principal residence
1340 Edward III rebuilt the castle
1547 Henry VIII born at Windsor
1642 Cromwell's troops occupied the castle to guard the road to London
1688 King William III had red deer sent from Germany to the castle's grounds
1770 Royal apartments couldn't be lived in due to neglect
1820 George IV began grand rebuilding of castle
1860 Royal Family spent Christmas at Windsor
1903 King Edward VII held grand ball at Windsor

SOURCE 11
The history of Windsor Castle.

C1350 *Castle built*
1488 *Castle used as base for rebellion against the king*
1528 *King James V of Scotland took control of castle*
1542 *Earl Douglas regained control of castle*
1651 *Cromwell's forces lay siege – cannon cause considerable damage*
1699 *Castle not fit to live in*
1890 *Restoration of Tantallon begun*

SOURCE 12
The history of Tantallon Castle.

SOURCE 13
Tantallon Castle, Firth of Forth.

attainment target 2

1. Why do you think different historians offer different reasons for the decline of castles?
2. Many people think all castles are ruined in battles or sieges. Why is this an unlikely reason for the destruction of castles?
3. If you had Source 8 only to go on, what would you think was the main reason for the decline of castles?
4. Does one or more of the historians' ideas in Source 4 to 7 begin to look more accurate than the other ideas?
5. When were the castles in Sources 11 and 12 last used in war?
6. Why did the castles in Sources 11 and 12 decline?
7. Do Sources 11 and 12 support any of the historians ideas in Sources 4 to 7?
8. Which do you think were the most important, and most common reasons for the decline of castles?

Castles today

Compare Source 14 with Source 1. Source 14 shows Ludlow Castle as it was in 1798. It was neglected and in a poor state of repair. However, today it has a completely new function. Like many other castles it has become a tourist attraction. Once more many castles are being well looked after. Walls are repaired. Ivy is removed. Rooms are labelled and guidebooks written. What was once both a home and a battleground now has a different life.

SOURCE 14

Ludlow Castle.

ACTIVITY

This is a whole class activity, which should be carried out only after you have studied unit 3 and unit 4.

Characters

1 The lord who owns the castle.

2 The lady. She could be the owner instead of the lord.

3 Steward. See unit 3 for important information on the jobs of the steward, chamberlain and butler.

4 Chamberlain.

5 Butler.

6 Marshal.

7 Children.

8 Other servants.

9 Visiting entertainers.

10 Visiting lord or lady.

11 Master mason.

12 People from the nearby town, with supplies to sell.

Action

The lord, and lady, are about to return to the castle after an absence of six months. There is food to be prepared, rooms to be got ready and a fire to be lit in the Great Hall. When they have arrived, the lord and lady, will call all the chief officials of the castle to give a report on what they have done during the lord's absence. The lord and lady will find out what their children have been doing. Then there will be a great feast in the Hall, perhaps with entertainment.

An important visitor, perhaps even the king or queen, is due to arrive. This is a great honour, but also causes great upheaval. The whole castle will have to be got ready and everyone will be involved in trying to make a good impression on the guests.

The lord and lady decide that their castle is rather outdated. They want to extend it, *either* to make it more difficult to attack (see unit 2), or to make it more comfortable (see unit 5).

They discuss their decision, and the other characters also discuss what they think is best from their point of view. Whatever they decide to do, they will need a master mason (see unit 4). It will also cost a great deal of money.

Timeline

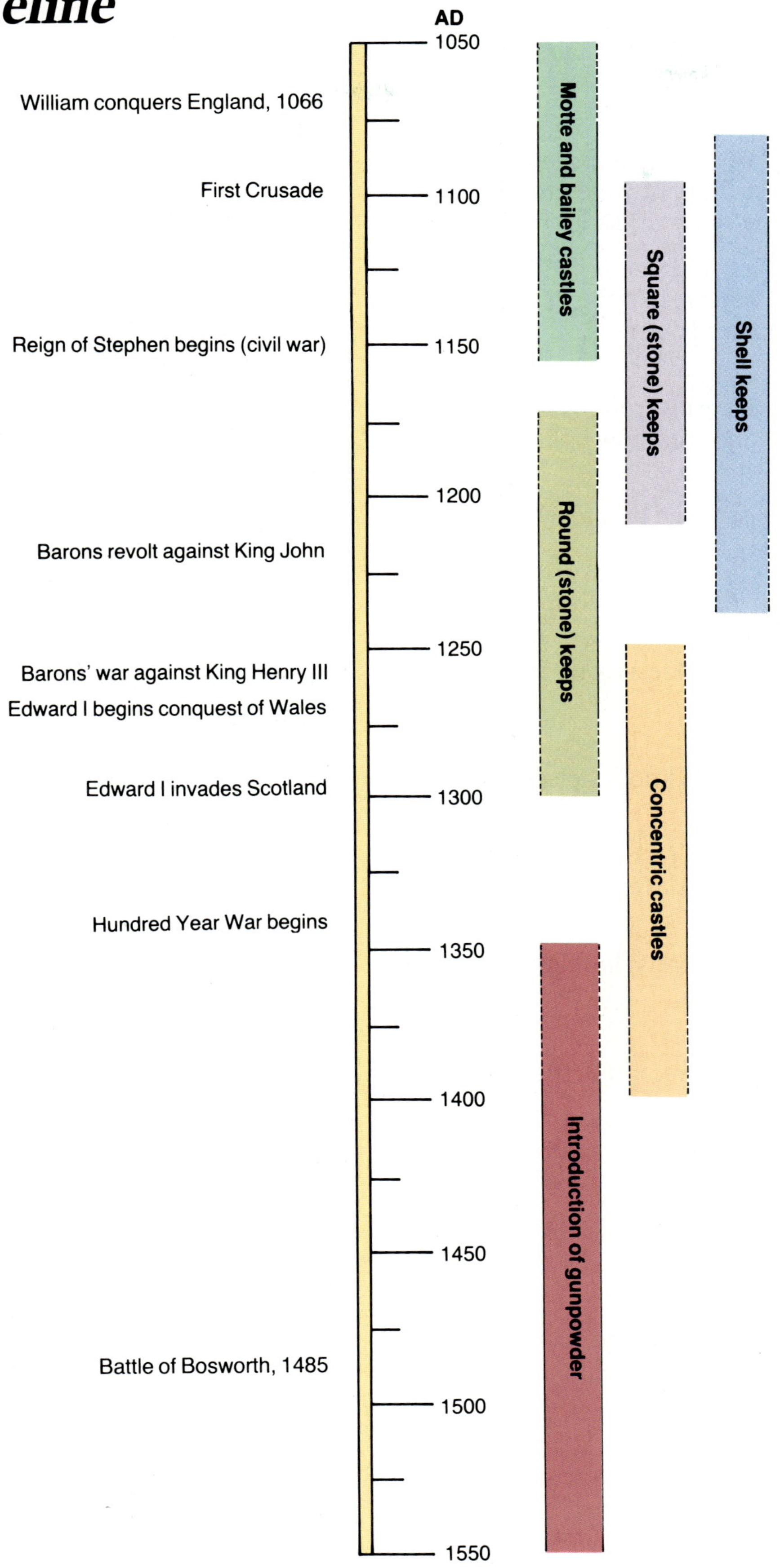
AD
1050
William conquers England, 1066
First Crusade
1100
Reign of Stephen begins (civil war)
1150
1200
Barons revolt against King John
1250
Barons' war against King Henry III
Edward I begins conquest of Wales
Edward I invades Scotland
1300
Hundred Year War begins
1350
1400
1450
Battle of Bosworth, 1485
1500
1550
Motte and bailey castles
Square (stone) keeps
Shell keeps
Round (stone) keeps
Concentric castles
Introduction of gunpowder

Glossary

Anglo-Saxon
People who lived in and ruled England before the Norman Conquest. They provided most of the labour to build the Norman castles.

Arms race
A contest, usually between countries, to become the strongest military power.

Arrow slits
Narrow holes in the walls from which knights could fire arrows and crossbow bolts.

Bailey
Castle living area enclosed by a fence.

Banker masons
Cut the stones for building.

Barbican
Double tower built outside a castle to protect the gate house.

Battering ram
Large tree trunk used to knock holes in walls.

Conscription
Workers forced to build castles. They were paid and were therefore not slaves.

Crenelations
Blocks built at regular intervals along castle walls to protect the defenders.

Crusade
Christian expedition to recapture the Holy Land.

Drop holes
Overhanging arches with open bottoms used to drop stones on attackers.

Fixer mason
Laid the stones in place.

Garderobe
Originally a wardrobe or private place that came to mean toilet.

Great hall
Main living and eating area of most castles.

Keep
The strongest part of the castle.

Mangonal
A gigantic catapult used to throw rocks.

Master mason
Chief builder in charge of all the workers, often responsible for designing castles.

Motte
The mounds, usually man made, on which early castles were built.

Normans
Followers of William the Conqueror, who invaded England in 1066 and began a massive castle-building programme.

Palisade
A wooden fence built around the outside of a castle or on top of the castle walls.

Scaling ladder
Ladder used for climbing over a wall.

Shell keep
Early Norman stone castles built without a strong keep.

Siege tower
Wooden platforms to help get over castle walls.

Trebuchet
A massive sling used to throw rocks.

Vault
Rounded stone roof.

Windless
Large wooden wheel, which worked like a hamster wheel, used to raise materials during castle building.

Index

Page numbers in **bold** refer to illustrations/captions

First published 1991 by CollinsEducational
77–85 Fulham Palace Road
Hammersmith
London W6 8JB

ISBN 0–00–327230 – 3

Cover designed by Glynis Edwards
Book designed by Glynis Edwards
Edited by Lesley Taylor
Series planning by Nicole Lagneau
Picture research by Marilyn Rawlings and Linda Proud
Artwork by John Booth and Angela Lumley
Production by Ken Ruskin

Typeset by Dorchester Typesetting Group Ltd.

Printed and bound by Stige-Arti Grafiche, Italy

Acknowledgements

Every effort has been made to contact the holders of copyright material but if any have been inadvertently overlooked the publishers will be pleased to make the necessary arrangements at the first opportunity.

Photographs The publishers would like to thank the following for permission to reproduce photographs on these pages:

T = top, B = bottom, R = right, L = left

Aerofilms 9R, 10; Aviation Picture Library 12L; Bridgeman Art Library 24/Victoria and Albert Museum, 45/British Museum; British Library 21, 25, 36TR, 42; Governing body of Christ Church Library, Oxford 19L; Collections, Roy Stendhall Humphryes 7T, 17B, 20; English Heritage 14, 18T, 22L, 23TL, 23TR; English Life Publications 30TL; Equinox, Oxford 30B/ Bibliotheque Nationale, Paris; ET Archive 15L/ Bibliotheque Nationale, 31B/Bibliotheque Nationale, 31T/Bodleian Library, Oxford, 34/British Library; Mary Evans Picture Library 16R, 19TR; Fotomas Index 27; Sonia Halliday 15R; Michael Holford 6, 17T, 18B; Angelo Hornak 38B; Hulton Picture Company 38T; Viscount de L'Isle VC, KG, private collection 28; A.F. Kersting 39; Leiden University Library 8; Mansell Collection 37; Osterreichische Nationalbibliothek, Vienna 29B, 35L; Patrimonio Nacional, Madrid 32; Photo Video 23BL; Pierpont Morgan Library 1991 26, 29T; Rochester District Council 9L; Scotland in Focus 43R; Skyscan Balloon Photography 11T, 22R, 43L; Frank Spooner Pictures 12R/Gamma; Still Moving Picture Company 44; Syndication International 40/ Britain on View; Trinity College Dublin 36BR; Welsh Historic Monuments 36L; Zefa Picture Company 41/E. Vetter.

Cover photograph: Skyscan Balloon Photography.